TUSCANY

THE HORIZONS OF ART AND BEAUTY

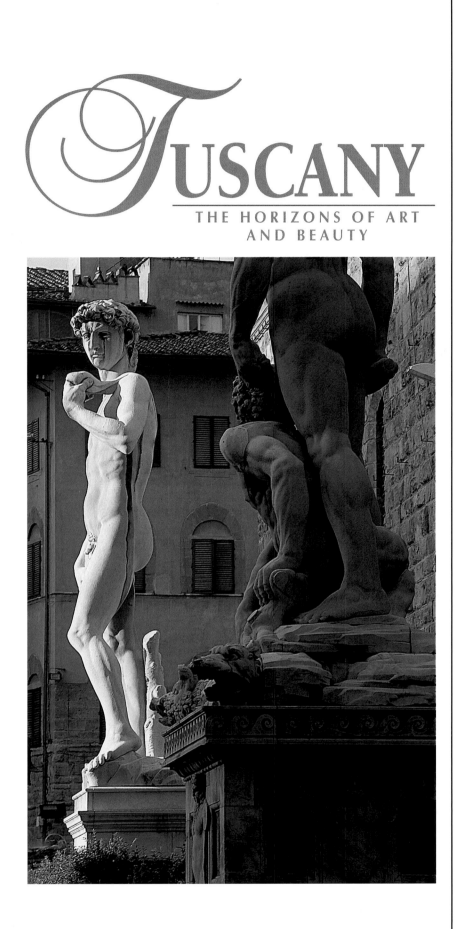

WHITE STAR
PUBLISHERS

TUSCANY

THE HORIZONS OF ART AND BEAUTY

Text
Chiara Libero

Edited by
Valeria Manferto De Fabianis

Graphic design by
Patrizia Balocco
Anna Galliani

Translation
Neil Frazer Davenport

CONTENTS

© 1995 White Star S.r.l.
Via C. Sassone, 22/24
13100 Vercelli, Italy
www.whitestar.it

ISBN 88-8095-777-5

Reprints:
 2 3 4 5 6   06 05 04 03 02

Printed in Italy

1 Standing at the main entrance of the Palazzo della Signoria welcoming tourists and visitors is the best loved Florentine statue, Michelangelo's David. The original is conserved in the Accademia delle Belle Arti.

2-3 The Torre del Mangia, the Duomo, the Campanile, the red roofs of the palazzi: the prodigious splendor of Siena is captured in a single shot.

4-5 The church of Santa Maria della Spina lays on the banks of the Arno in Pisa. Threatened by periodic flooding, the church was demolished during the last century and then reconstructed.

6-7 The Ponte Vecchio
in Florence is known
throughout the world as the
goldsmiths' bridge because
of the craftsmen who have
traded there since the time
of Cosimo I.

8-9 Cypresses are one of
the characteristic elements
of the Sienese landscape.
They line the twisting roads
and the crests of the hills,
delineate the meadows and
fields, and often constitute
the only tall plants in the
region.

10-11 The silhouettes of
cypresses, symbols of the
Sienese countryside, emerge
out of the morning mist
near Asciano.

INTRODUCTION

How difficult it is to write about Tuscany. One is swamped by the tritest of clichés to the point where it seems impossible to find even a single phrase that has not already been used by an art historian, a poet, a naturalist, an anthropologist, or an ordinary, casual visitor. There is a certain magnetism about Tuscany, and there must be very few people, Italian or otherwise, who have not at some point exclaimed "Oh, how I'd like to live in Florence!," or "how I'd love a cottage in the Chianti hills!" Mention the "Sienese countryside" and up pop idyllic images done to death by the advertising industry: long twisting roads cutting through bright green fields punctuated by vineyards and beautiful stone farmhouses, a pair of grazing horses or perhaps a village inhabited by cheerful farmers and fairy tale peasant girls, not to mention the greatest of Tuscany's friends, those foreigners for whom the Grand Tour has never gone out of fashion. Following in the footsteps of Byron, Dickens, Rogers, Wordsworth, and Forster, they return in perhaps less sophisticated, but decidedly more numerous and worldly groups.

They overlook the myriad incongruities, the erratic museum opening hours, the pizzas served in front of the Palazzo della Signoria, the panini offered in Piazza del Campo and even the tacky, illuminated plastic reproductions of the Leaning Tower of Pisa.

They could hardly return to Hamburg, Minneapolis, or Osaka and say that yes, they wanted to take a look at Tuscany, but their time was up after Rome and Venice. For Italians, on the other hand, Tuscany is a rather distant "mamma," almost too beautiful and famous. She is not arrogant by any means, willing as she is to put herself on show and invite us to share in her riches, but nevertheless well aware of her position. In contrast with Rome, torn between her imperial glory and the trattorie of the Trastevere, between ministerial limousines and Cinecittà, between nobility and "the people," and in contrast with Venice where the tourist industry has succeeded in destroying the magic, Florence has preserved its essentially provincial character. Ready to welcome, it is just as quick to close in on itself and be content with its glorious past, its brief tenure as capital under the Savoias, and even more content to have returned to its role as Queen of that most peaceful, photographed, painted, and described of lands. With its crown of art cities and less obvious, but nonetheless brilliant, minor gems with its harsh, rocky islands and generous but occasionally treacherous mountains, and with that musical language with its beautifully judged accents and tones Tuscany is enchanting.

Although Italian was created here, the Tuscans speak a language of their own, the full range of which no imitator could ever hope to reproduce. It is the language of a deep-rooted culture, one so charming as to grace each and every one of the region's inhabitants, making them all, if only for an instant, Dante's favorite grandson.

13 Massive and soaring, forming part of a monumental complex of extraordinary power, Santa Maria del Fiore is, with its Brunelleschi dome and the Baptistery, the spiritual center of the city.

14-15 The Uccellina Mountains constitute two thirds of the Maremma Natural Park, a wild unspoiled oasis, a maze of trees and shrubs in which the only signs of man's passing are the ruins of the watchtowers.

16-17 Pitigliano, in the Maremma, high on an outcrop of tuff, has Etruscan origins but was at its peak in the Middle Ages as a fief of the Aldobrandeschi and the Orsini.

18-19 Fluttering in the wind is the symbol of the Goose, one of the seventeen neighborhoods in the town of Siena that compete, in July and August, with feverish intensity for victory in the Palio, a traditional centuries-old horse race.

THE STONES
OF HISTORY

20-21 The Torre del Mangia and the Duomo, the symbols of Sienese civic and religious power, stand out against the clear night sky.

*A*t the turn of the century the young Lucy Honeychurch, armed with her faithful Baedeker guide, arrived in Florence with very clear intentions: to take a room with a view at the Pensione Bertolini, experience Italian art at first hand and, if at all possible, have an adventure. What kind of an adventure she did not know. What she did know is that only in Florence could her thirst for life and beauty be satisfied. Lucy was following in the footsteps of thousands of Britons, Germans, and Americans, all traveling on the Grand Tour, the indispensable finishing touch to the education of any well-bred young person of the era. Arriving in Tuscany in those times must have been very different. The search for decent accommodation, a reliable driver, and a restaurant themselves constituted an adventure. But have things changed so very much since then? No, not really. Tuscany and its art cities, large and small, are still essential sights. Adventures are still there to be experienced by those with a spirit open to beauty, harmony, genius, and the unusual. And, all things considered, the search for a good hotel is still something of a gamble. The grand tours are still arriving from Britain, Germany, and America, and now also from Japan and the rest of the world. Today, they are brisker, more worldly, and occasionally (but not always) better organized.

The first stop is always Florence: perhaps out of respect, perhaps for the sake of convenience.

The trains drawing into Santa Maria Novella Station and the buses parked in Piazzale Michelangelo daily disgorge thousands of tourists eager to devour Florentine Madonnas and Della Robbia babies.

They put up with the indescribable humidity of the summer, the interminable treks, and the lines at the entrances to museums.

How could one return to Bonn or Osaka and admit to not having seen the Tondo Doni, or not to have gasped at the climb to the top of the Campanile, Giotto's Tower? The tour is completed with the aid of a variety of history of art guides and novels, risking to overload the intellect at the expense of the heart and imagination.

Weighed down with the writings of Ruskin, Browning, Stendahl, and Goethe, it hard to believe that this is a living city, and not a miraculous relic of the Middle Ages and the Renaissance. Florence is of course a city that relies heavily on tourism, but it manages to treat it as something that has fallen into its lap by chance. So much so that the last visitors to be received with authentic joy and relief were the youngsters armed with sleeping bags who arrived in that tragic November of 1966 to save Florence's masterpieces from the fury of the flooding Arno.

Far from allowing themselves to be overwhelmed, the Florentines regard the "three-day trippers" with a hint of derisive insolence. It is in fact perhaps true to say that for the modern Florentines, historic Florence is more of a burden than a source of revenue and international fame, like an inheritance that is difficult to run and to administrate. As early as the 1950's that acute observer Mary MacCarthy wrote: "History, for Florence, is neither legend nor eternity, but a massive weight of rough building stone demanding continual repairs, pressing on the modern city like a debt, blocking progress."

However, if the Florentines of the past had decided that progress was not for them, what language would be spoken in Italy today? What masterpieces would people be able to admire in the museums and galleries? What would be the state of political and social developments on the peninsula? While not wishing to load the descendants of Dante, Giotto, and Machiavelli with too much responsibility, it is nonetheless true to say that nothing is further removed from the Florentine spirit than the concept that art, beauty, and great ideas are the fruit of a sacred respect for tradition.

Florence, the offspring of Rome in the Middle Ages, a second Athens during the Renaissance, has always shied away from mere supporting roles inventing, century after century, its own identity and exporting it with pride. One of the characteristics most typically Florentine is that of looking beyond one's own horizons. The "castrum" founded by Fiorinus, one of Julius Caesar's generals, guarded the consular roads leading to Rome, Lucca, Pisa, and Faenza. This laid the basis for future trade and diplomatic missions. Their journeying led the Florentines to accept and export ideas and products, while still maintaining a precise identity and a desire to return to their homeland. Above all they demonstrated a subtle and at times insidious insolence towards the established order, with a distinct preference for argument and brawling, or at least for a cruel joke.

22-23 The Florentine monuments form part of our collective consciousness. Palazzo Vecchio, Brunelleschi's dome, and Giotto's Tower are part of humanity's patrimony, visited by millions of tourists but still capable of arousing profound emotion.

This is what history, stories, and literature have taught us and from the clashes with the other Tuscan cities and from the perpetual struggles between the rival factions.

Nor did Florence ever suffer from a sense of inferiority to Rome, the cradle of civilization.

The proclamation by which in 1296 Arnolfo di Cambio was entrusted with the construction of the Duomo as a replacement for the old church of Santa Reparata was clear in its intentions. Florence wanted a building capable of exceeding in dimensions and magnificence anything that had been created in the golden ages of Rome and Greece. Anything more explicit is hard to imagine.

Although the resulting building cannot match the majesty of the Parthenon, the beauty of Santa Maria del Fiore is breathtaking, thanks in part to the additions by Giotto and Brunelleschi. A cardinal point and the ideal beginning to any tour, the Duomo can even be seen from the highway, an apparition which forms part of the collective consciousness not only of the Italians but of the entire world. It is a cardinal point of the city, but by no means its only attraction. Those intent on visiting the whole of Florence should dedicate more than the three days of the typical all-inclusive tour.

The museums alone number around sixty. Each church is a museum in itself. And, there are the palazzi, the bridges, and the picturesque streets. So much for Baedeker!

One risks an overdose of art, a full-blown case of Stendahl's Syndrome. Florence could be just too much for visitor with refined and broad-based, but not inexhaustible interests. No lesser personage than Henry James, who was certainly no inexperienced loafer, had to admit to being a little overwhelmed.

A glance at a map of the Florentine monuments is enough to give one an idea of the challenge involved. Taking into account just the historic triangle formed by the Fortezza da Basso, San Marco Square, and the Forte di Belvedere, excluding therefore Fiesole, San Miniato, Le Cascine Park, and the more modest quarters, there is not a single street, turn, or piazza which fails to provide at least one feature worthy of note. However, this in a city which could never have been accused of wanting to turn itself into a permanent museum. Even though the mass of tourists has stimulated the proliferation

of bars and fast food joints, souvenir stands, and crib-guides with their "must see" lists, Florence remains a place in which people live, work, and enjoy activities other than the "systematic skimming" practiced by the tourists. This is a characteristic which is thankfully shared by all the great Tuscan cities of art.

If one follows the course of the Arno almost to its mouth, as far as Pisa, a great, historic and unfortunate rival to Florence, one finds something of the same spirit. Although the Pisans boast wonders which people throughout the world can recognize, they themselves have above all been great travelers, traders, and academics.

Pisa was also situated on the routes of two great consular roads, the Aurelia and the Emilia Scauria, which linked it with Rome, Provence, and as far off as the Baltic. But first and foremost it had one of the two ports fundamental to traffic on the Mediterranean: a source of great wealth, not only in financial terms. The monumental complex of the Campo dei Miracoli with the Duomo, the Campanile, the Baptistery, and the Camposanto would itself be sufficient to ensure Pisa's eternal glory.

The image of the Leaning Tower is in all probability one of the ten most famous in the world. It is a universal symbol, albeit one devalued by the countless plastic reproductions which transform it into ash-trays, paper weights, clocks, and tacky ornaments, and make of it a classic example of tourist kitsch. An idealized link between heaven and Earth, the Tower was erected in a seafarers' town. Nowadays, the Tyrrhenian Sea seems a long way off, separated by a 6 mile stretch of river. And yet Pisa still retains a vague saltiness in the air.

This very salt is responsible for the corrosion of the marble on the facades of the churches.

The smell of the sea blends with that of the river which here, in contrast to Florence where it rushes past, appears resigned to its impending fate. Everything is more relaxed, although history has not spared Pisa its dramatic moments of great political success and severe defeat.

The years between 1000 and 1300 witnessed prodigious development both in the city itself and in the surrouding region. Having become a great maritime power, Pisa celebrated its triumphs with

24 Diosalvi conceived the Baptistery at Pisa as a grandiose circular temple, with the exterior imaginatively subdivided into three increasingly light orders: blind arcades on columns and arched loggias perforated like fine lace.

25 The foundation of the Tower dates back to 1173 and is attributed to Bonanno. The design called for a much higher tower than the current one (circa 180 feet) but subsidence, cause of the famous lean, forced the adoption of a more modest structure.

26 bottom The Baptistery of Pistoia, built between 1338 and 1359, according to plans by Andrea Pisano, is an elegant Gothic structure with an octagonal base, and covered with white and green marble. In this picture, one can see the upper section of one of the three portals, all of which are decorated with finely worked statues, reliefs in white marble, and geometric decorative motifs.

a series of illustrious monuments, and saw its population rise to the notable total of 40,000 inhabitants. It was only following the defeat against Meloria that decadence set in through wars, the loss of its independence, shortages, floods, and epidemics.

A sequence of tragedies which would have brought any civilization to its knees. At least in Pisa, now isolated inland, the memories of its greatness remain. Apart from the Campo dei Miracoli (a bizarre name, given that in the Middles Ages the piazzas so called were the theaters of charlatans and tumblers), the list is impressive. There are numerous churches, palazzi, piazzas, and wonders like Santa Maria della Spina, a pale and minuscule Gothic jewel, a triumph of spires and stone carving, which in the second half of the nineteenth century was completely demolished and reconstructed in identical form a few yards further back to save it from continual flooding.

Pinnacles and steeples are often found in Pisan architecture as a kind of indelible symbol, a perpetual memorial to an all too brief and intense golden age. The bitterness of defeat was attenuated to some extent by the fame, even abroad, of the city's university. The Pisan institute, "Lo Studio," was the first to be given official recognition with the Papal bull "In Supremae dignitatis" from Clement VI in 1343. The tradition of Pisa as a seat of learning continued and with the "Scuola Normale," founded by Napoleon in 1810, the city was again at the forefront of higher education. The tradition had far reaching roots. Apart from the oft-cited Galileo Galilei and his experiments into the isochronicity of the pendulum in the Duomo, Pisa is linked with a veritable legend of the world of mathematics, Leonardo Fibonacci. Fibonacci identified a series of numbers of very precise proportions (each being the sum of the two preceding figures) which could be found in countless natural phenomena. It is hard to say whether anything of his geniality still remains in the city, but what is certain is that one of its current assets is represented by its students, who arrive not only from all over Italy, but also from abroad. Thus, for thousands of years, Pisa has remained a young, broad-minded city.

Pisa retains a cosmopolitan tradition which led a scandalized prelate in the times of Matilde di Canossa to declare: "The city is contaminated by pagans, Turks, Libyans, Parthians, and dark-skinned

26-27 The unusual form of the Campanile of the Duomo at Pistoia (above, a detail) is the result of the vicissitudes that have marked its history. It was first a Lombard tower, then the civic tower, and only took on its present form in the sixteenth century.

27 top The Duomo at Pistoia, characterized by an elegant colonnade with glazed terracotta vaults by Andrea Della Robbia, was begun in the fifth century and rebuilt with significant modifications in the thirteenth century.

27 bottom Giovanni Pisano left two works of extraordinary emotive and artistic impact in the church of Sant'Andrea at Pistoia: a wooden crucifix and, above all, the pulpit with deep relief carvings illustrating the story of the redemption.

Chaldeans wandering the beaches." Clearly, racial and religious contamination was not frowned upon by the Pisans, but rather treated with indulgence. A great influx of foreigners meant great mercantile and maritime success. The wider the horizons, the richer the harvest of ideas. Today the tourists remain alongside the students, but are however excluded from the lives of the permanent guests. The Pisans, like the Florentines, maintain a detached distance between themselves and those who believe that they can get to know their city in just a few hours. Less forthcoming and more discreet, the Pisans only ever let themselves go on particular occasions such as the "Gioco del Ponte," once decidedly violent but now somewhat tamer. At these times the combative spirit of eight centuries ago when the struggles were against Amalfi, Genoa, and Venice, reappears and the Pisan character gets heated.

There is an international air at Siena too, despite the rather paradoxical fact that this is perhaps one of the most tenaciously provincial Tuscan cities.

In the case of Siena this is by no means a pejorative term, but rather an affectionate description of a civic life-style that has somehow survived, at least in part, the delusions of history.

Isolated, and of an almost absolute medieval purity, it has often been asked what it is about Siena that has, for motives that occasionally appear unjust, prevented modernity from making any more than minor incursions within its walls. And, above all, it is asked why, at a particular historical moment, in this particular place, blessed by a series

28 top The cathedral at Arezzo enjoys a magnificent setting and is approached by a flight of steps. The theme is continued inside with frescoes and large stained-glass windows and culminates in Piero della Francesca's Magdalen.

28 bottom The earliest surviving work by Cimabue, the Crucifix, *is conserved in the church of San Domenico. The bright colors and the pain-wracked face inspire a profoundly emotional religious charge.*

29 The thirteenth century church of San Francesco is a veritable gallery of art. In the choir the remarkable fresco cycle by Piero della Francesca dedicated to the Legend of the True Cross *provides a resumé of the themes of renaissance painting.*

of fortunate circumstances, a school of painting was created which boasts at least four names fundamental to the history of art: Duccio di Buoninsegna, Simone Martini, and the two Lorenzettis. This phenomenon rocked the art world from the thirteenth century to the Renaissance, and can perhaps be explained by the character of the Sienese themselves. The adjectives which have, over the centuries, been applied to them are countless and often contradictory: bizarre, versatile, chivalrous, sentimental, free, heroic, gay, and dramatic.

The Florentines, who never got on with the Sienese, said with a touch of malice that their character was inherited not from the Romans, who are considered to have founded the city, but from the Gauls led by Brenno, or the uncivilized Germanic barbarians. Whatever its origins, the Sienese character is one of intense collective pride, the best expression of which is to be found in the "Palio delle Contrade." It is also revealed in art that lavishly indulges in gold and color, with energy, mystic ecstasy, and proud celebration of civic glories, demonstrated in the Good Government cycle by Ambrogio Lorenzetti. In Siena art has always been a public triumph.

Duccio di Buoninsegna's last brush stroke on the Maestà was the signal for three days of collective celebrations. Today it still seems that the detachment of man's artistic creations from the lives of the city's inhabitants is less accentuated at Siena than elsewhere. Perhaps the merit is due to its compact dimensions and essentially medieval layout.

Siena, like a well-fed snail, fills every nook and cranny of its shell, it turns away cars, invites visitors to walk and climb the steps of San Giovanni, and to wander with the wafting scent of the spices used to flavor the "panforte."

Coming in from the country, the yellow-ochre Crete and the green hills, the terracotta red of the buildings, the campanili, and the slim Gothic shapes seem perfectly integrated, almost spontaneous outcrops of the land. In fact, city and country exist in a symbiotic relationship at Siena, and one senses that below the herring-bone pattern cobbles of the Campo the city's three hills converge. One also senses that the shell-like form was not the result of some planner's whim, but rather derives from a precise geomorphologic structure. There is little sense in discussing Siena and only mentioning Piazza del Campo in passing, and not only because Montaigne rightly (with all due apologies to the Venetians) defined it as the world's most beautiful piazza. What is more important is that Piazza del Campo is a concentration of Siena's civic history, often combined with elements of its religious history which finds its focus higher up in the massive bulk of the Duomo. The market was held in the Campo. In the past as it still does today, water arrived in the Campo to feed the Fonte Gaia via a 16 mile long aqueduct. But above all, the Campo was the area for those games for which the Sienese went literally crazy. The Palio was of course the most famous, but there were also more bloody and fanciful contests which reflected, in a sporting light, those which took place outside the city walls against enemies rather less inclined to fight. The oldest and perhaps the most bizarre was that of the "pugna," a form of boxing, the aim of which was simply to beat the living daylights out of one's opponent. Then there was the "Mazzascudo" game in which contestants with wicker baskets on their heads beat one another with the active participation of the spectators. Mortal injuries were no more than unfortunate consequences of the game.

"Panem et Circenses," as the Roman ancestors had taught, holds true in Siena. The Sienese passion for sports has always been so intense that, as legend has it, it was they who taught the Spanish, long-term dominators, the rules and customs of bullfighting. It is a city always ready for a joke and demonstrating intense passion, but also capable of heart-stopping delicacy. Siena is irresistible at dusk on a summer's evening, as the sun slowly sinks behind the towers and roofs tinting the terracotta an even deeper shade of red. It is this curious blend of violence and harmony, rage and affection, which makes Siena a city of exquisite memories for all.

The three Tuscan "capitals," Florence, Pisa, and Siena, are flanked by a court of regal princesses. Lucca, Arezzo, and Pistoia, and also Grosseto, Livorno (Leghorn), Massa, and Carrara, are often overlooked in the lists of the great cities of art. Lucca certainly merits the closest of attention, not least because it represents the last resting place of the beautiful, beloved Ilaria del Caretto, wife of Paolo di Guinigi, nobleman of the city. Her tomb has won the

31 top left Little of the original Sienese style is left in the Duomo at Grosseto. The facade was completely rebuilt in the first half of the nineteenth century. While the interior has also lost its original structure, you can still admire an attractive font and altar dedicated to the Madonna delle Grazie by Antonio Ghini.

31 top right Grosseto, the Cinderella of Tuscan cities, has hidden surprises for those who look further than the imposing walls which enclose the oldest part of the town, and which in the nineteenth century were converted to a public walkway.

31 bottom In the ancient heart of the city, enclosed by the walls, extends Piazza Dante, once known as the Cisternone or the Piazza of the Chains. The city is relatively young, being founded after the year 935 when the ancient Roselle was devastated by the Saracens and was definitively abandoned in favor of the small castle of Grosseto.

hearts of generations of romantics, but unfortunately has also attracted the attentions of vandals armed with pencils and, more recently, felt-tip pens. Jacopo della Quercia, sculptor and in this case exceptional portraitist, captured all her composed grace and serene beauty. These could also be the adjectives most suited to Lucca, a tranquil elderly lady, protected by imposing and seemingly impregnable city walls. Behind its turrets the city has changed very little, preserving a character which falls somewhere between the noble and the affable, a somewhat neglected minor capital. The best loved street is undoubtedly Via Filungo, civilly (and also inevitably given its dimensions) reserved for pedestrians. The street could justifiably be compared with the Mercerie in Venice, but which in spite of the opulence of its shop windows, also has something in common with an eastern souk. It is incredible to think that over a century ago Lucca risked seeing its structure obliterated: in 1866 the city walls were put up for sale, on offer to private building speculators. They were bought by the town council and there were plans in the air for some time to demolish them to make way for some unknown project. Fortunately the citizens protested, thus saving one of the most suggestive walks in Tuscany.

Provincial enough to make it a haven for numerous exhausted city-dwellers, a stone's throw from some sublime countryside and punctuated by extraordinary villas, Lucca is and always has been a wealthy town of traders and bankers.

The height of its economic, political, and artistic power came in the thirteenth century, when the Lucchese began to acquire a reputation for being astute and intelligent merchants. Well aware of their inability to compete with Florence in fields such as wool, they specialized in silk. Their damasks, velvets, and gold and silver brocades were famous throughout the medieval world, enjoying success in France, Flanders, and England. The Lucchese exported textiles, but also citizens. Numerous important Lucchese families were to be found in Paris, Montpellier, and the Champagne region, and they played a vital role in improving relationships between the European potentates.

This was of course the period of greatest artistic splendor in the town. The Romanesque style of Lucca is a blend of solidity, simplicity, and a desire for

32-33 The completion of Duccio da Buoninsegna's **Maestà** (the illustration shows a detail of the reverse side of the panel), today kept in Siena's Museo dell'Opera Metropolitana, was the starting point for three days of festivities involving the entire city. A masterpiece of Sienese painting from the sixteenth century, the **Maestà** is a complex and fascinating creation and soon became a model for other compositions on the same theme.

clarity. Only later did the influence of Pisa introduce more extravagant forms.

This was also the beginning of a love-hate relationship with Florence. Allies when it suited both parties, but more frequently enemies, Lucca was destined to submit, to turn in on itself, and to concentrate on defending its very existence, improving civic life and increasing trade.

However, conflicts and conspiracies were not lacking at Lucca either, such as the celebrated case of the "Burlamacchi." It is as if to say that when foreign policy is disappointing, there is always internal strife to fall back on. Were it not so, how could one bear such perfect peace in which strolling a couple of miles outside the city walls plunges one into the paradise of Lucca's surrounding countryside. The outlying villas merit a chapter to themselves. Like the Venetian villas of the Riviera del Brenta, they represent the wealth, good taste, and desire for entertainment of the good citizens who, exhausted by the cares of business, had monumental masterpieces erected for their vacations. The most celebrated examples are Villa Mansi at Segromigno, dating back to the sixteenth century but rebuilt two centuries later by Juvara, Villa della Gattaiola, Villa Orsetti, and Villa Torrigiani.

Equally tied to the land and the countryside, Pistoia is a town which has experienced few moments of grandeur and numerous episodes of defeat. The anonymous chronicler of the "Istorie Pistoiesi" writes of dark times in which conflicts and sectarian strife transformed the town and its countryside into a theater of massacres until 1306 when it fell to the Florentines. At that point the massacre extended to the works of art, and as the spirit of revenge died forever, it left in its place a sober melancholy. The conquerors destroyed all evidence of the former power, demolishing the towers and the city walls.

The Pistoiese tried to resist, but with little success, and early in the fifteenth century they became in practice the subjects of the neighboring city.

Perhaps this is why among all the Tuscans they are the least concerned with celebrating their past.

They prefer to forget. The "Giostra dell'Orso," revived following the Second World War after centuries of neglect, has no precise historical references. Here they prefer to treat the Duomo, the beautiful Romanesque, churches and the compact medieval nucleus as integral parts of civic life, rather than as treasures there to be fawned over.

Yet the art of Pistoia is by no means second rate. Beginning with the works left by Coppo di Marcovaldo, now recognized as the teacher of Cimabue, one can admire a great crucifix in the Duomo. In the fourteenth century Giotto had a powerful influence on artists even out here in "provincial" Pistoia. Then there is the Romanesque architecture, the Gothic style of the Baptistery, and the church of San Paolo. But Pistoia is above all a town of sculpture. In particular, the pulpit by Giovanni Pisano in the church of Sant'Andrea is an eternal symbol of recognition and devotion to the city that had taken in the artist. It is a work in which, as Pietro Toesca writes, "form is given to that 'visible speech' which Dante cherished in sculpture. No constriction tied the hand of the sculptor, even in the brief spaces afforded by the pendentives of the arches, in imagining those figures in acts which create complex harmonies, which collide with one another in a physical and spiritual agitation so intense as to refute comparison with any other masterpiece of Gothic art. The torments of the inner life appear to be the only factors determining the composition and form of each group and each figure, not through outward stylistic conventions, but through the expression of movement and passion." A long citation for a work composed only a little before the city's defeat, and which perhaps sums up the contradictory nature and spirit of the Pistoiese, destined to live unwillingly in the shadow of Florence.

The last stop on our imaginary tour of metropolitan Tuscany is Arezzo, which Giorgio Saviane has defined as "concentrated Tuscany": from the limpid, petrified purity of the art of Piero della Francesca to the immortal salacity of the "damned" writings of Pietro Aretino. Unfortunately modern town planning has eroded a great deal of the appeal commented on by the travelers of some decades ago. The changes have also affected the town's economic structure, with the arrival of important industries such as those of gold and clothing. The changes do not, however, obscure the noble origins of the city. Arretium was one of the most important Etruscan cities, home of one of the twelve "lucumonie."

Wealthy and in a privileged position for trade,

35 The original of Michelangelo's David is housed in the Galleria dell'Accademia in Florence where it is protected not only from the pollution in the Piazza della Signoria which threatened to ruin it, but also from attacks by vandals similar to the affront it suffered at the hand of a madman in 1991.

at the head of the three valleys of the Arno, the Tevere, and the Chiana, Arezzo had all the right credentials to become a center of fundamental importance.

This promise was fulfilled during the period of Roman domination, and was conserved through to the Middle Ages when civic life became more intense, in the shadow of the Lombards and the Marchesi of Tuscany, with the foundation of a law and literature school, closed in 1300. But like all Tuscan cities Arezzo is above all a city of art.

And the personification of the city is Piero della Francesca with his rigorous perspective, classical monumentality, and the Legend of the True Cross, the cycle of frescoes in the choir of the church of San Francesco. It is enough to look at a detail, the view of Arezzo, and to compare it with the mosaic of the city roofs to understand the degree to which the artist was in tune with the commission, and above all how he brought to it his own idea of crystalline clarity.

The Legend is a work of maturity. The medieval stories of Jacopo da Varagine become episodes of the Renaissance, solemn exaltations of the concrete and the human, a sober and discreet nobility which is also a feature of the city's streets. Unfortunately the beauty of the ancient town center was disrupted during the last world war by tragic destruction, often compounded by examples of ill-judged building developments. The monumental zone has survived isolated and vainly protected by the sixteenth century fortress. Below the fortress, in Piazza Grande, the "Giostra del Saracino" is held in late summer and is, together with Siena's "Palio" and the Florentine "Historical Calcio," the most popular of the region's colorful traditional festivals.

36-37 The Sleeping Child
*is one of the most famous
works by Giovanni Duprè,
a nineteenth century
Sienese sculptor, follower of
Canova, and champion of
the neoclassical style. In his
autobiographical writings
Duprè described in a clear,
lively style, the Tuscan
artistic milieu of his era.*

FLORENCE, OF ARMS AND BEAUTY

38 The campanile of Santo Spirito, in the foreground, announces the panorama of roofs, domes, and towers which makes the aerial view of Florence an ambassador for Italian life and culture throughout the world.

38-39 Before it became the "realm" of the goldsmiths, the Ponte Vecchio was the meat market. The butchers were evicted definitively at the end of the sixteenth century with the charge of having besmirched the beauty of the site with the by-products of their trade.

40 *The immensity of Santa Maria del Fiore, the Baptistery, and Giotto's Tower is counterbalanced by the extraordinary delicacy of their decorations and the prodigious perfection of their proportions.*

41 Civic might is expressed in the great religious and secular buildings. In the shadow of the Duomo and the Palazzo Vecchio the city prospered, struggled, and became the capital of art.

42 bottom The Giardini di Bóboli, behind the magnificent Palazzo Pitti, were the work of Tribolo and Buontalenti. They represent one of the most felicitous examples of the Italianate garden.

42-43 The Arno has played a precise role in history of Florence, and thus in the changes which led to it becoming a great center of art. It was in fact the Arno which supplied water to the wool and leather industries from which the wealth of the medieval city was accumulated and which financed works of art.

43 top The Baptistery of the Duomo, dedicated to San Giovanni, has been perhaps one of the best loved Florentine monuments ever since the times of Dante.

43 bottom The bridges spanning the Arno have not enjoyed an easy life, battling against the fury of floods as well as human perfidy. During the Second World War they were all mined with the exception of the Ponte Vecchio.

44-45 "In Santa Croce with no Baedeker" is the title of a chapter in Forster's A Room With A View. *Without a guide it is by no means easy to find one's way around the works of art which transform the austere church into an extraordinary gallery, the funeral monuments which inspired Foscolo, and the chapels containing masterpieces such as Donatello's* Crucifix.

46-47 Just a few steps away from the railroad station, Santa Maria Novella, one of the most famous churches in Florence, offers a remarkable sampling of Gothic architecture. Work on its construction began in 1249, plans were drawn up, and construction was directed by an architect from the Dominican order of monks until the work was completed in 1360.

The facade of the church constitutes a true indication of the skills of the master decorators. Even Leon Battista Alberti worked on the church. He designed the portal, which was completed between 1456 and 1470, and all of the material that stands above the handsome central cornice, including the two delicate lateral volutes.

48 It was Cosimo I who, in the second half of the sixteenth century, commissioned Giorgio Vassari to design the Palazzo degli Uffizi destined, as the name suggests, to house the judiciary and administrative offices. The building today holds the State Archives and, above all, the Galleria, probably one of the most famous and most visited art galleries in the world.

49 There are several dozen museums in Florence. The Museo di San Marco (top, left) is housed in the splendid convent where Fra' Angelico left a good number of his works. In the galleries of the Palazzo Vecchio (top, right) the Medici era can be relived, while the Galleria dell'Accademia (bottom) is visited above all for its great Michelangelo masterpieces such as the dramatic Pietà da Palestrina.

50 As in many other works by Leonardo da Vinci, the landscape in the background of the Annunciation *was based on a reality as seen and transformed by the eye of a genius.*

51 *In the age of Dante, Cimabue, the author of the superb* Madonna in Maestà, *(now in the Galleria degli Uffizi), was considered to be a proud, arrogant, and self-important man. However, his works have an extraordinary expressive force with an agitated rhythm that relaxes in the faces of his saints.*

52-53 *For a long time
Sandro Botticelli was
considered to be a prophet of
beauty. But with the* Birth
of Venus *and* Primavera
*he renders his conceptions
in a symbolic, problematical
painting linked to the neo-*
*Platonic culture. Thus, his
naked Venus is a symbol of
the simplicity and purity of
nature and faith, while*
Primavera *removes itself
from reality in order to go
beyond it and enter into the
complex world of allegory.*

54-55 *The* Tondo Doni *(conserved in the Uffizi) and the* Pietà *(in the Museo dell'Opera del Duomo) represent two fundamental moments in the career of Michelangelo Buonarroti. The* Tondo *is an early work based on the play of light with mellow tones. It has recently been returned to its original splendor after being seriously damaged in the 1993 explosion which devastated part of the Galleria. The* Pietà*, executed in the artist's prime, demonstrates his movement away from the formal sculptural models of ancient art towards a more personal and searching form of expression.*

56 Palazzo Medici-Riccardi, built by Michelozzo in the mid-fifteenth century, was the home of Cosimo il Vecchio, Lorenzo il Magnifico, Charles VIII of France, and Charles V of Spain. Imposingly elegant, the house was the renaissance prototype of the noble residence.

57 The Cappella de'Pazzi, in one of the cloisters of Santa Croce, was one of the last works by Filippo Brunelleschi. The artist was by then a master of his art and the formal perfection is rigorous, severe, and articulated by chromatic contrasts.

58 Piazza Santissima Annunziata, the most harmonious square in Florence, features two elegant baroque fountains completed by Pietro Tacca in 1629. This pictures shows a detail.

59 In Florence no one calls the Neptune Fountain by Bartolomeo Ammannati by its proper name. The Biancone as it became known failed to arouse much enthusiasm among the citizens, and in fact an irreverent rhyming verse was soon coined which ran "Oh Ammannato, oh Ammannato, what beautiful marble you've ruined."

60-61 *The most famous piece of Florentine sculpture, the* David *in Piazza della Signoria, was Michelangelo's vision of a beautiful, taut, and physically perfect youth, created by the sculptor at the height of his power.*

62-63 *Time has not been gentle with the Ponte Vecchio. Originally it was a wooden construction which was destroyed by a flood in 1333. In the middle of that same century, Neri di Fioravante erected the stone bridge which was* *damaged by the retreating Germans at the end of the Second World War and then in the floods of 1966. Today it is one of Florence's best loved symbols, dutifully crossed by same tourists on the look out for bargains in the myriad jewellers' shops.*

Siena, the Effect of Good Government

64-65 *From above, one can better appreciate the incredible urbanistic homogeneity that distinguishes Siena. The color red can be found in the pavement of the Campo, Siena's remarkable shell-shaped central square, in the roofs of the houses, and in the bricks of the ancient, battlemented* palazzi, *among them the exquisite Palazzo Sansedoni, built in the years*

around the end of the thirteenth century and the beginning of the fourteenth. Nobles and commoners have always enjoyed the same rich scene of beauty, the same fine materials, and the same handsome unity of thought and purpose: to preserve their city's square as one of the world's most renowned abodes of the spirit.

66-67 *It is here, between Piazza del Campo and the Duomo, that the public part of the Palio delle Contrade takes place. And the Sienese, in spite of their fiercely proud attachment to the quarter in which they were born, recognize the fundamental role played by both the symbolic monuments in the urban and social fabric of the city.*

69 The story behind the building of the Duomo was long and complex and culminated in a unbuilt design for a grandiose extension which would have made the existing building the transept of the new cathedral. The work as it appears today is a synthesis of diverse designs including that of Giovanni Pisano, the author of many of the statues gracing the facade.

68 top left A reminder of the city's Roman origins, the Sienese wolf with the two twins sits on the top of a column in Piazza del Duomo.

68 bottom left The majority of the statues executed by Giovanni Pisano for the facade of the Duomo are now kept in the Museo dell'Opera Metropolitana to counter the ravages of time. However, the lyricism and vivacity of the artist remain intact, together with an intensely dramatic religiosity.

68 right The Campanile of the Duomo of Siena, constructed in 1313 to the design of Agostino di Giovanni and Agnolo di Ventura, features multi-colored marble decoration echoing the hues of the cathedral body.

70-71 The mosaics, executed by the Venetian Castellani in the second half of the nineteenth century, are similar to those of the Duomo at Orvieto and represent episodes in the life of the Virgin Mary, culminating in the Coronation.

71 The opulent facade of the Duomo, animated and graceful in spite of the weight of the central rose window, was begun by Giovanni Pisano at the end of the thirteenth century and completed by Giovanni di Cecco after 1376, drawing inspiration from the Duomo of Orvieto.

72 left The starry sky, the gilded angels, frescoes, stucco, and multi-colored marble: decorative riches are concentrated on the magnificent ceiling of the cathedral.

72 top right This enchanting picture of the interior of the Duomo, or Cathedral, emphasizes once again its grandeur and mass, highlighted by the faint daylight that envelops the exquisite mosaics.

72 bottom right The pulpit by Nicola Pisano and his collaborators was sculpted between 1266 and 1268. The narrative structure is rich and lively, characterized by great dynamism and drama of a decidedly Gothic nature. Statuary and architecture combine in an immensely expressive work.

73 The interior of the cathedral with its forest of pillars creating fantastic perspectives can at first sight leave one dazed and confused. The bands of black and white marble, the gold, the plethora of decorations and paintings, and the intricate pavement overwhelm the structure of the building while providing visitors with a concentrated summary of medieval art.

74 In his Maestà, *conserved in the Palazzo Pubblico in Siena, Simone Martini revisited the theme and composition tackled by Duccio di Buoninsegna, adding a touch of humanity and a more mobile, rarefied light to the stately perfection of the maestro.*

74-75 Duccio di Buoninsegna painted the monumental Maestà (now in the Museo dell'Opera del Duomo) for the high altar of the Duomo at Siena. This large composition represents the most grandiose work on wood panel of the Middle Ages. Its choral sacredness, freshness, and spirituality made it a fundamental model for the artists of the era.

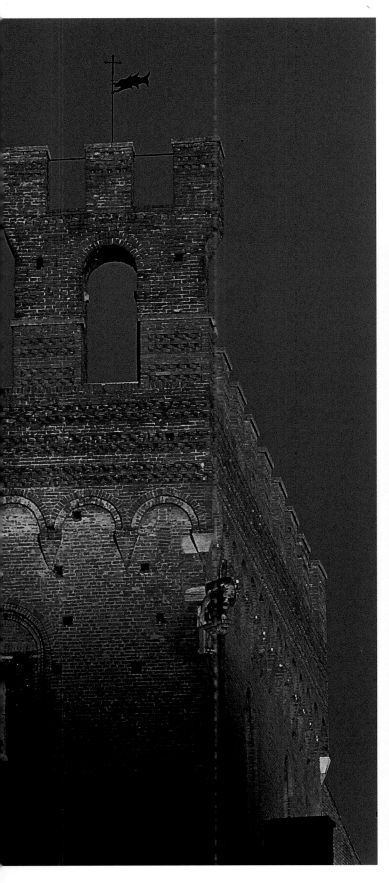

76-77 Of Siena's Palazzo Pubblico, it has been said that it synthesizes the architecture of all the fourteenth century palazzi *of the city which, in one way or another, all owe a debt to its example. It forms a perfect backdrop to the Campo, one of the world's most beautiful squares.*

77 Remarkably tall and slim, the Torre del Mangia was added to the body of the Palazzo Pubblico in 1338, with the construction being entrusted to the Perugian brothers Minuccio and Francesco di Rinaldo. The belfry crowning the tower is the work of Lippo Memmi.

LUCCA, TO THE MEMORY OF ILARIA DEL CARRETTO

78 The mosaic on the facade of the church of San Frediano is traditionally attributed to the school of Berlingheri. It depicts the Ascension of Christ *and can be read like the illuminated page of a precious medieval missal.*

79 The church of San Michele in Foro is located on the former site of the Roman forum. The richly decorated facade is an excellent example of Pisan-Lucchese Romanesque: a perfect thirteenth century scene.

80 top The tomb of Ilaria del Caretto by Jacopo della Quercia lays in the Duomo at Lucca. The young wife of Paolo Guinigi, a nobleman of the city, is portrayed in all her beauty, surrounded by putti *and with her favorite dog at her feet. Affection and loss seem to have been perpetuated over the centuries and this is still one of the best loved and most visited monuments.*

80 bottom Its uniqueness derives above all from the variety of stylistic, architectural, and decorative features that have been utilized. The marble tiles, the smooth and carved columns, and the asymmetry determined by the successive addition of the campanile all make it a fascinatingly original work.

80-81 The Duomo at Lucca, dedicated to San Martino, has a long and glorious history stretching back to the era of San Frediano in the sixth century. It was later rebuilt by Anselmo di Baggio, but assumed its definitive form in the thirteenth century.

PISA, WEALTH AND CULTURE IN THE SHADOW OF THE TOWER

82 Behind the Duomo stands the Campanile, the Leaning Tower. Medieval records reveal that the tower soon gave cause for concern and that attempts to compensate for the subsidence began at the end of the thirteenth century.

82-83 Pisa's magnificent monumental complex, the Duomo, the Tower, the Baptistery, and the Camposanto, bears witness to the historic wealth of the city. The fate of the Campanile, which has always suffered from the effects of subsidence, has the world holding its breath.

83 bottom Buscheto's genius, said to be responsible for the Duomo at Pisa (the photo shows a detail of the apse), developed in an ambient rich in classical references, open to the influence of Eastern culture and extremely advanced from a technological point of view.

84-85 According to recent research, the elements of the Piazza dei Miracoli are arranged according to precise cosmological symbolism linked to the constellation of Aries, with the Duomo, the Baptistery, and the Tower representing the principal stars.

86 *The shapely dome of the Duomo at Pisa rests on a high tambor and is considered to be the first example of an "extradosal dome." Like the cathedral itself, it is thought to be the work of Buscheto who rests in a tomb located below one of the arcades of the facade.*

87 *The vibrant chiaroscuro typical of the Pisan arcades is developed in a thousand different ways on the monuments of the Piazza dei Miracoli.*

88-89 *Lined by sober palazzi, the banks of the Arno at Pisa are symbolic of the composed dignity of the city as the great river prepares to conclude at the Tyrrhenian Sea a journey begun on the Falterona uplands.*

MASSA, CARRARA AND LIVORNO, CITIES OF MARBLE AND SEA

90 top Even the palazzi *that stand in the center of Massa speak of a pomp and wealth that reflect the glorious past of the town.*

90 bottom Capital of the Duchy of Massa and Carrara in the sixteenth century, prior to the eleventh century Massa was just a small rural center which only developed following the decline of the nearby Luni. It first belonged to the Malaspina family of Fosdinova, and then the

Cybo-Malaspina family who gave it its definitive plan. Massa Cybea, with a regular grid plan, saw the building of palazzi *and churches, and above all the large red* palazzo *which in the eighteenth century was decorated with stucco, grotesque carvings, and floral motifs.*

91 top The Mastio di Matilde shows above the massive walls of the Fortezza Vecchia at Livorno. It dates back to the eleventh century, but its origins go even further back. It was built on the site of Roman ruins in the first century before Christ.

91 bottom The imposing Porto Mediceo at Livorno was built between 1571 and 1618. The port benefited from a system of duty-free re-exportation of goods held in bond. In 1675 it was declared a free port, a move which increased the prosperity of the city on the Tyrrhenian Sea. To the right runs the sea front. It recalls Leghorn's past maritime splendors with the opulent grace of the Umbertine buildings lightened by the esplanades and terraces facing the open sea.

San Gimignano, Ancient Symbol of Power

92-93 Thanks to its strategic position clinging to a hillside dominating the Val d'Elsa on the Via Francigena, in the Middle Ages San Gimignano enjoyed a golden age. But the rivalry between the various noble families, in particular the Ardinghelli Guelphs and the Ghibelline Salvucci, led to the explosion of tragically bloody struggles. The towers were thus in reality veritable fortresses set one in front of the other: a memento of past splendors but also of tragedy and mourning.

94-95 *The interior of the Collegiata at San Gimignano is decorated with splendid frescoes: on the left, a detail of Ghirlandaio's* Story of Santa Fina, *on the right* Scenes from the Life of Christ *by Barna da Siena.*

CYPRESSES
VILLAS AND
VILLAGES

96-97 Montalcino, in the
Val d'Orcia, is celebrated
throughout the world for
its wine "il Brunello."
Of relatively recent origins,
the Brunello is exclusively
produced from Sangiovese
vines, and the best vintages
attract remarkable prices.

Set between the Alps and Sicily, between North and South, featuring mountains and hills, open valleys and narrow gorges, Tuscany is more than just art. Tuscany is countryside so characteristic that the phrase "a Tuscan landscape" is also used to describe that of Umbria or the Marche. The Chianti hills, the Sienese Crete, the Mugello, the Maremma, and the Garfagnana are not simply ideal backdrops to a thousand towns and villages. They are an indispensable part of their appeal, inseparable from the work of man.

There was a strong temptation to start to describe the least cherished, most mistreated and overlooked area, the bleak Maremma. Instead, it joins the narrative after taking leave of Tuscany from the haven of Monte Argentario after having been welcomed by the Mugello, an immense lake of green forests bordered by the Apennines and crowned by Monte Falterona, source of the "fiumicel" as Dante called the Arno. Entering Tuscany by this route must have gladdened the hearts of the travellers of bygone times. It is a landscape of hills, knolls, villas, and fortresses, the favored retreat of the Florentines who, from the late fourteenth century, had astutely swept away the feudal strongholds of the Guidi and the Albertini, transforming the Val di Sieve into an oasis of peace. The Medici were originally from this area and indulged themselves in such idle pursuits as hunting and feasting. The proximity and dominance of Florence also deprived the Mugello of its native heroes. Few now remember that Giotto, Fra Angelico, and Andrea del Castagno were from the Mugello, eternally annexed as they are by the city. It is of some consolation to visit regal villas like that at Cafaggiolo, built for Cosimo il Vecchio near Barberino, or the village of Scarperia, famous for its knife-making crafts. One then moves on through Fiorenzuola, with its "Rocca," or fortress, and city walls designed by Sangallo, to Borgo San Lorenzo, the "capital" of the Mugello. An ancient castle dedicated more to commerce than to defence (it still hosts a lively weekly market), and featuring the superlative "Pieve" (parish church) di San Lorenzo which boasts a Madonna attributed to Giotto. The Mugello extends almost infinitely into a landscape full of color which brings one to Vespignano, considered to be the birthplace of Giotto and said to be the site of his historic meeting with Cimabue, and to Vicchio, home of Fra Angelico.

It is certainly not difficult to imagine a scene so crucial to the history of art set among the "pievi,"
the hills punctuating the route towards Dicomano. This is the land of painters in which the style that made Florence great was formed and nurtured. The woods make marvelous rambling country and one can clamber up the knolls in the hope of spying a hidden monastery, or one of the rare castles to have survived to the present day.

Lost sensations are there to be discovered among the myriad shades of green which vary with the seasons.

To the south of the Mugello the Casentino extends in an almost unbroken sweep, straddling the border between Tuscany and Emilia. This is the upper Arno valley, and Dante was the first to remark on its impressive beauty and cool climate, so different to the torrid heat of Florence. However, despite its pleasant appearance, the tempestuous battles which have over the centuries shattered its tranquillity, certainly did not escape the poet's notice. The very name of the Campaldino plain, theater of the victory of the Florentine Guelphs over the Ghibellines of Arezzo, or that of Anghiari is sufficient to evoke memories of pain and blood. Fortunately, this is also a land of great artists, from Piero della Francesca to Michelangelo to Paolo Uccello, and great spirituality. Monte della Verna, for example, belonged to an incorrigible medieval Don Juan, Orlando Cattani of Siena, who could hardly have dreamed that an insignificant, ragged monk would overturn his life. The monk in question was Francis of Assisi, visiting the San Leo castle in Romagna. Orlando heard him speak, was converted, and subsequently presented him with the entire mountain. Francis and his followers, with the help of their benefactor, raised a church on La Verna where he later received the stigmata. Today the Verna Sanctuary is a monastery, library, museum, and even a meteorological observatory.

The origins of the Camaldoli monastery also lie in a story of patronage. On this occasion, the protagonist was San Romualdo, who a little after the year 1000 was given permission by Maldolo of Arezzo to build on the ruins of a castle. The monks of Camaldoli were fundamental to the diffusion of knowledge in the Middle Ages. Locked into their hermitage, bound by a severe order, they copied codices long before the advent of the printed word simplified matters, and in the early sixteenth century they founded an important press. Immersed in the woods, La Verna and Camaldoli are true oases of peace.

Art, on the other hand, is to be found in the numerous towns and villages, with due homage being paid to Pratovecchio, birthplace of Paolo Uccello, and

99 In the summer the Tuscan countryside explodes with color. The yellow of the sunflowers and the ochre of the Crete are unforgettable and are identical to those depicted by the great medieval and Renaissance artists.

100-101 Set among the
rolling Sienese hills is the
church of San Biagio, designed
by Antonio da Sangallo the
Elder. The golden travertine
stone stets off the
harmonious simplicity of the
building set on a knoll below
the town of Montepulciano.

100 bottom Bernardo
Tolomei, the founder of the
Abbazia di Monte Oliveto
Maggiore, was inspired by
the desolate, overwhelming
solitude of the Crete. Far
from political and public
cares, he retired here to
pray and study.

the neighboring parish of Romena, the most important in the Casentino valley. One should also pause at Poppi, the favorite residence of the Guidi family.

The Castello dei Guidi, an evocative remnant of the Middle Ages, is a still formidable symbol of secular feudalism, and it makes one wonder what impact its bulk may have had on the enemy forces. It would appear, in fact, that the Palazzo della Signoria in Florence is a simple copy, even though there are those who claim that the current flowed in the opposite direction and that it was the victors who exported their style to the area.

The last stop is at Cortona, a fascinating city to say the very least, blessed by an invaluable artistic heritage and virtually unchanged from the Renaissance to the present day. First and foremost, there is the magnificent Santa Maria al Calcinaio, then San Domenico, embellished with superb paintings, the Duomo, the remains of the Etruscan fortifications, the Palazzo Pretorio, and the Museo Diocesano. Even a stroll along the paved streets, browsing in the antique shops, can be enchanting as one is transported back in time. Tuscany can also be entered via other mountains, such as the Lunigiana overlooking the baroque, medieval town of Pontremoli with its old houses with slate roofs and the splendid castle housing the archaeological museum, custodian of the Luni civilization. The statue-like stele pose countless unresolved mysteries. Were they idols? Marker stones? Funeral stones? No one knows. Curiosity is combined with unease in this portion of land which is Tuscan in name, but which still retains

101 A few miles out of Siena, the Castello delle Quattro Torri stands in magnificent isolation. Built between the fourteenth and fifteenth centuries, the castle is very similar to the Este family's castle at Ferrara built at around the same time.

102-103 The Val d'Orcia frequently offers panoramas like this one: gentle, rolling hills crowned by an occasional cypress grove silhouetted against the skyline.

104-105 Man has always intervened to model, delimit, and render more fertile the Tuscan countryside. In the area around Siena even the rural dwellings are magically integrated into the landscape.

something of Emilia and Liguria. Descending from Pontremoli towards the sea along the road halfway up the hillside, to the right the landscape is dark and brooding, while to the left are the sunny "pievi" and castles. This was a tempestuous region with around 30 castles, and over 150 fortified houses and watchtowers. However, it has redeemed itself admirably with culture. The Bancarella literary prize, awarded each summer in the Piazza della Repubblica in Pontremoli, is an event crucial to taking the pulse of Italian readers, while the booksellers' town par excellence is Montereggio, immersed deep in the

countryside. The inhabitants of this valley have roamed the world for four centuries founding book shops and publishing companies. The area is under the jurisdiction of the Massa-Carrara province. While Massa is a prevalently modern town, albeit with a historic medieval nucleus huddled around the fortress, Carrara is synonymous with marble, and not only in Italy. For centuries the precious material on which entire pages of the history of art have been written has been extracted from the quarries in the Carrione valley. Marble has been the source of the area's wealth for at least two thousand years, and the entire Apuane landscape bears the scars of mining, furrowed as it is by the canyons and by the white blazes of the waste tips. A blessing for the economy of the area, but one which Carrara has paid for in terms of an industrial appearance, redeemed by the occasional attractive seventeenth-century palazzo, and above all by the Romanesque-Gothic Duomo.

Leaving the city behind, one climbs the steeply twisting roads towards Colonnata or Fantiscritti, and from the road one can see the great scars where Michelangelo quarried the marble for the statues in the Medici chapels and the tomb of Julius II.

From here, passing by way of the Pian della Foiba, one enters the Garfagnana where, much against his will, Ariosto spent unhappy years as Governor on behalf of the Estes. Narrow valleys dense with oaks lead to Castelnuovo, Coreglia Antelminelli, Bagni di Lucca, and the delights of Barga, beloved of Giovannino Pascoli, and on to the Grotta del Vento, which works wonders for the lungs. Here great art is

106-107 The villages of Colonnata and Torano serve the surrounding marble quarries. Set like outcrops in a rocky landscape, they have always been tied to these rich yet grudging mountains which concede their wealth only to those with the expertise to mine their slopes of white gold.

107 The marble quarries which dominate the village of Campo Cecina on the Apuane hills have supplied the material on which immortal pages in the history of art have been written for two thousand years.

diluted by the domestic familiarity of the poetry learnt by heart in Italian primary schools, and the memory of a well-known and much maligned poet. But each village has a Romanesque church, a terracotta, a crucifix, or a pulpit worthy of a visit. On occasion, as in 1994, one may have the good fortune to come across a relic of the past which has survived intact. When Lake Vagli, created by a hydroelectric dam, was drained, the drowned village of Fabbriche di Careggine reappeared. The mute roads, the roofless church, and the abandoned houses came back to life for a few months before being submerged once more in the

tranquil silence of the Garfagnana. One descends rapidly from the Apuane mountains to the plain and then to the sea. First the Versilia coast where the old fishing villages of Forte dei Marmi, le Focette, Pietrasanta, Camaiore, and Viareggio have become part and parcel of the summer entertainment industry, while often retaining something of their aristocratic detachment. Following the coast one enters the territory beloved of Puccini, Torre del Lago, the expanse of Lake Massciuccoli and the wonderful presidential estate of San Rossore. After just a few miles, however, the green pine woods give way to the port of Livorno, also known as Leghorn in English. For those not born here, this is a difficult city to love. Built facing the sea but simply, without drama, uncompromisingly "un-Tuscan," and with no attractive quarters, its lack of impressive structures is perhaps due in part to its uniform layout (and its relative youth). Reliable records of its existence date back no further than the fourteenth century when a miniscule fishing village existed on the site where the Medicean port was to be founded. The vicissitudes of the city, among which was a brief period of subjection to Genoa, had had little effect until 1530 when, under the dominion of the Medici, Livorno became the most important port in Tuscany. Its demographic expansion began in the seventeenth century. The city attracted considerable immigration both from the rest of Grand Duchy and from abroad, and it guaranteed religious freedom for all.

This was a truly remarkable act and made Livorno one of the few earthly "paradises" for Jews, a situation unique in Italy which was to last until the age of Napoleon I, and which saw the birth of great "leshivòths" and even its own language, Bagito.

The great synagogue, considered to be among the most beautiful in Italy, was destroyed and it has recently been replaced with an unremarkable temple.

The fame of Livorno as the city of freedom began to grow from the seventeenth century. The foreign population soon reached 35% of the total.

Great political ferment was also stimulated in a similar fashion, thanks to industrial development which from the nineteenth century concentrated an increasingly numerous proletariat around the port. Livorno is the city of the International Workers Association, the Universal Democratic Alliance, the Bacunian Anarchists and the Socialist Congress which, in 1921, saw the birth of the Italian Communist Party.

108 top The ruins of the Abbazia di San Galgano, set in the midst of the countryside, are one of the most evocative Romanesque monuments in the Sienese area.

108 bottom The Abbazia di Monte Oliveto Maggiore houses superb frescoes by Luca Signorelli and Sodoma, considered to be among the most important works of the Renaissance.

108-109 For some years now the Abbazia di Sant'Antimo has once again echoed to the sound of Gregorian chants thanks to five French monks who have dedicated themselves to the order and the upkeep of the abbey.

109 bottom The wealthy Abbazia di Monte Oliveto Maggiore, one of the grandest in Tuscany, looks out over the Sienese Crete. The abbey was founded in 1313 by Giovanni Tolomei, a master of Law at the Sienese Studio who abandoned wealth and honor in favor of a Benedictine monastic life with a special interest in art and science.

The inhabitants of Livorno still retain a reputation for being less than peaceful, but ever ready for a joke. It is worth recalling the ferocious trick pulled by three students just a few years ago when they totally hoodwinked massed ranks of experts with their claims that the fragments of stone they had modeled with an electric drill were actually original Modigliani sculptures. The whole world laughed and Livorno applauded. Tricking their neighbors, taking pride in their own individuality, well removed from the other Tuscans with even their own dialect, they are contrary to nature in these parts. Even though it is some distance away, well off shore and down a bit towards the south, the Tuscan archipelago also belongs to the province of Livorno. The seven islands of varying sizes are the summits of seven Apennine peaks, submerged and separated from the mainland millions of years ago, although legend would have it that they were created when the necklace of the Venus of Tyrrhene broke, scattering the gems of which it was composed. Those precious stones gave rise to Elba, Gorgona, Capraia, Pianosa, Montecristo, Giglio, and Giannutri.

It is said that Jason during his wanderings with Medea sailed into the bay of Elba where today stands the port of Portoferraio. Elba was in fact well known in ancient times when the Ligurians and the Greeks exploited its iron ore deposits a thousand years before Christ. The Romans, on the other hand, were more interested in its wines, even though Virgil described it as "insula inexhaustis chalybum generosa metallis." Iron and "tourism" have thus alternated in the economic and political history of Elba up to the present day, with the significant historical interlude of the 300-day imprisonment of Napoleon.

More isolated, and perhaps still more fascinating, the other islands have enjoyed diverse destinies. They have often been the refuges of monks, hermits, and lovers of silence, meditation, and prayer, as can be seen from the ruins of the small monasteries left on Giannutri and the magnificent Montecristo, but also the strongholds of the various conquerors to have alternated over the course of the centuries, from Pisa to the Appians to the Medici. Montecristo, where Dumas set Edmond Dantès' hunt for treasure, is today a protected wildlife reserve after having once been the private hunting grounds of Vittorio Emanuele II. All the islands are veritable natural paradises, from Pianosa, a tormenting source of anguish for convicts, to

111 Monteriggioni (left) and Certaldo (right): two diverse destinies for two medieval villages with important roles in history and literature. Monteriggioni, isolated on a hill top, supports itself in its splendid decline through tourism and nostalgia, virtually shunning any contact with modernity. Certaldo, the birthplace of Francesco Boccaccio, has on the other hand adapted with the times to become an important industrial center.

110 Sadly, typical rural dwellings in the Val d'Orcia are occasionally allowed to fall into disrepair. For some years now, however, the cottages have become the preferred prey of both Italians and foreigners who buy and restore them to an oasis of holiday peace and tranquility.

112-113 Sorano, in the province of Grosseto, dominates the Lente valley from a rocky spur. The compact village center retains a markedly medieval character, exemplified by the tower-houses and the imposing Fortezza Ursinea.

114-115 Pitigliano also perches on an outcrop of tuff, and a fine white wine is produced on the surrounding hills. In the past the village housed a large Jewish community.

116 top Montepulciano (in the photo, the Palazzo del Comune) is one of the most typical sixteenth century towns. Its appearance was radically changed by the work of Antonio da Sangallo, with significant contributions also made by Michelozzo and Vignola. On a smaller scale, the Palazzo del Comune is inspired by the style of the Palazzo Vecchio in Florence.

116 center The current form of the ancient Vallambrosana abbey of Passignano, near Tavernelle Val di Pesa, dates back to the seventeenth century. The interior is decorated with works by Cresti, Alessandro Allori, Butteri, and Veli.

the volcanic rocks of Capraia and the gentle beaches of Giglio which alternate with stretches of rugged cliffs. Their destiny has always been that of the struggle between exploitation and the perhaps unconfessed desire to remain detached, beautiful, and isolated, almost untouchable.

Returning to the mainland, and moving away from the sea on the road towards Siena, the underground wealth of the area once again takes pride of place. Between the Cecina and Ombrone valleys extend the Colline Metallifere (the Metal Hills) with names which all evoke the fires of hell. The Luciferian blow-holes of Larderello lend the landscape a lunar aspect, and the ancients were convinced that the snorts came straight from the depths of Hades. Today the cylinders of the cooling towers and the steel pipework conceal much of the natural phenomena. Fortunately Volterra is close by, "an eagle's nest in precarious equilibrium," isolated among hills that concealed treasure: copper, lead, silver, and rock salt. Volterra was already important in Etruscan times, the ancient Velathri, one of the twelve "lucomonie," with huge, imposing walls, traces of which still remain. The Middle Ages, on the other hand, saw the city clinging to its castle, huddled around the Piazza dei Priori. But thanks to the underground resources and its strategic position, it was destined to succumb to the power of the neighboring cities. As usual, Florence triumphed and immediately imposed its presence installing the bulky Fortress, used as a prison. Volterra resigned itself to its destiny and it still appears to be waiting for its destiny to be fulfilled today. In the surrounding area, the phenomena of landslides on the hillsides, the dreaded "Balze," have already swallowed up cemeteries, villages, and Etruscan walls. An ancient Camaldolese abbey of Saints Justus and Clemente is now threatened, while another, now abandoned, is awaiting its fate. The future of the Chianti appears more tranquil. It is a region embodying the very essence of natural harmony in which man's activities are integrated in perfect symbiosis. It enchants with its undulating hills patchworked by vineyards, cultivated fields and farms, and punctuated by avenues of cypresses, villages, and valleys which take their names from the rivers running through them. The mosaic proves unforgettable and unmistakable for anyone granted even the most fleeting of glimpses. The Florentine nobility retreated to the Val

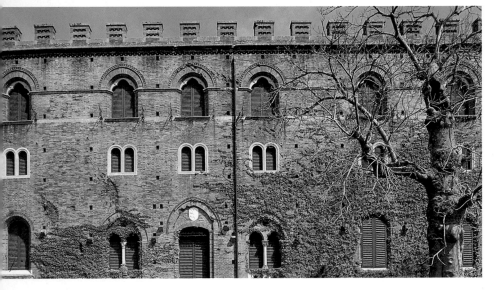

116 bottom On an isolated knoll on the slopes of the Chianti region stands the magnificent Castello di Brolio, home to one of the most famous wine producers of the area, Ricasoli. It was Bettino Ricasoli, an expert in agricultural matters, who invented the Chianti "formula": a blend of Sangiovese, Trebbiano, Malvasia, and Canaiolo grapes.

117 In the small, evocative village of Collodi, birthplace of Carlo Lorenzetti, the author of Pinocchio, Villa Garzoni stands out as an ideal model of the aristocratic villa, complemented by a garden begun in the mid-sixteenth century by Marquis Romano Garzoni and perfected in the seventeenth century by Ottaviano Diodati.

di Pesa for their vacations, and in the area around San Casciano, at Sant'Andrea in Percussina, Machiavelli found a haven from the cares of politics, dining with the local dignitaries: the baker, the notary, the miller, and the innkeeper. He enjoyed simple life favored by the climate, the greenery, and the shade of the cypress avenues. Val d'Elsa also appears suited to idleness with its knolls and the harmonious profiles of its hills. And yet, it is not lacking in memorials to proud combative moments. Boccaccio, born here at Certaldo, said that the waters of the Elsa had the property of turning bodies to stone and that it was dangerous to immerse oneself in them. What is certain is that along its course have arisen cities of stone.

San Gimignano is famed for its towers, although few remain compared with the seventy-odd which are said to have graced the town during its golden age.

San Gimignano was an important and wealthy trading point on the Via Francigena and in spite of its current decadence it remains one of Tuscany's historic sites, not only for its artistic treasures but also for that perfect landscape, that view which from on high extends in all directions, encompassing hills, villages, and meadows. There is no rhetoric in saying that here Father Time hesitated, undecided as to whether to proceed or to freeze, immobile. The two triangular piazzas, Piazza Cisterna and Piazza Duomo, are indispensable openings in a maze of streets and tall buildings, and feature the Collegiata (with frescos by Benozzo Gozzoli and Taddeo di Bartolo, and the **Annunciation** by Jacopo della Quercia), the Palazzo della Podestà, and two important museums with

collections of masterpieces of Florentine and Sienese art. San Gimignano is the most enchanting welcome to the Val d'Elsa imaginable, but it is not the only attraction. It is but a short drive to Colle Val d'Elsa, another product of the wealth created by the Via Francigena, but one with a rather different vocation. Only a fragment of the medieval town remains, set high above in contrast to the more "modern" section below. Further down the valley, ever since the Middle Ages, a network of canals has carried water to the wool and paper mills. The wealthy and faithful Colle made no great drama out of submitting to the might of Florence and

120 *The Abbazia di Vallombrosa has ancient origins. The first stones were laid by the hermit Giovanni Gualberto, who founded the Benedictine order of Vallambrosani, and who was canonized at the end of the twelfth century. It returned to active life only after the Second World War, following a history of mixed fortunes.*

121 There is more to the Chianti than just vineyards. There are also hidden monasteries and old country houses immersed in the luxuriant greenery. This location is close to Castellina, between the Pesa and Staggia valleys.

122-123 In the Balze of Volterra, the sudden shifting of the clayey ground, has over time swallowed up churches, houses, and convents. Today many historic buildings are still threatened by seemingly inevitable destruction.

continued to prosper and enrich itself with works of art. A completely different destiny awaited Monteriggioni, a village virtually straddling the border between Val d'Elsa and the Chianti hills. It was early in the thirteenth century when the Sienese decided to acquire a small hill from the nobility of Staggia in order to create a fortress capable of intimidating the omnipresent Florentines. This was a large, forbidding castle for its time, with a closed ring of stone, reinforced by fourteen towers. It is still awe-inspiring today, so isolated and brooding, protected by the Romanesque-Gothic church dedicated to Our Lady of the Assumption. From the peak of the hill one looks out over the Chianti hills, that marvelous synthesis of nature and the work of man, where even agriculture appears graced by art. The rural homes have an enchanting simplicity, and even the roads trace patterns far removed from the usual anonymous grids. The landscape has been modeled since the Middle Ages, adapting terrain that was not always so gently accommodating, such as the already mentioned "Balze" in the Volterra region, and beyond Siena, the Crete that occasionally degenerate into a harsh, lunar ruggedness. The Chianti region is thus not so uniform as one might think, although it is possible to clearly define the Chianti Classico wine producing area, which includes the Arbia, Pesa, and Greve valleys as far as the Val d'Orcia. The area does have an identifying symbol however: the cypresses which dot the countryside, emphasize the ridges of the hills, and appear in the paintings of the great artists. Cypresses and vineyards, fortresses, castles, villages, "pievi," and abbeys: even an elementary list of the attractions would be lengthy. The

suggestive area around Sovicille, for example, is rich in "pievi," castles, villages, and villas. On the rounded hills of the Sienese Montagnola there are spiritual havens such as the Agostinian hermitages at Lecceto and San Leonardo al Lago, or the beautiful Romanesque church at Ponte allo Spino. Not far away, the Romanesque style is again in magnificent evidence in the grandiose, solitary and imposing Sant'Antimo abbey, a few miles from Montalcino. The abbey appears at the foot of a valley like a mirage, lovingly cared for by five French monks who fervently practice the Gregorian rite. Those visitors who wish to

124 Close to Coreglia Antelminelli, a famous holiday retreat in the Garfagnana, there are numerous small villages which appear to be as close to the past as they are to the present day, surrounded by the dense green woodlands.

124-125 The Turrite stream in the Garfagnana flows past the village of Turrite Secca. Harsh and isolated, the area can throw up unexpected oases of greenery in the valleys between the high rocky mountains.

125 bottom From Barga, the artistic jewel of the Garfagnana, one can look out over the lush countryside punctuated by rustic cottages. Among its treasures the village boasts the beloved house of Giovanni Pascoli, a precious example of the privileged bourgeois lifestyle of the last century.

126-127 "The serenity of the air settled over everything like a morning dew," wrote Federigo Tozzi about the Sienese countryside which nothing seems to disturb.

128-129 The bell tower of Monte Oliveto Maggiore seems to emerge directly from the fog that mantles the Sienese hills.

experience the illusion of time travel can take part in the services. The sung mass on Sunday is not to be missed. Just as evocative are the San Galgano Abbey, the ruins of which are to be found open to the sky in the midst of the countryside, and the fortified abbey of Monte Oliveto, set in the Sienese Crete and surrounded by a dense cloak of hollies and cypresses. Luca Signorelli left an imposing memorial to art here as did Sodoma.

The entire area is rich in artistic testimony. Above all there is Pienza, "born out of a idea of love and a dream of beauty," as Pascoli wrote. It was Pope Pius II, Aenea Silvyus Piccolomini, who had the inspired, insane idea of transforming his birthplace, the little village of Corsignano, into a Renaissance utopia, the ideal city. Thanks to Leon Battista Alberti and Bernardo Rossellino, in just three years the dream became reality. The old medieval layout was swept away, and space was made for the cathedral, with a plain, bare interior so as not to interfere with its architectural perfection, and Palazzo Piccolomini with its loggia overlooking the Val d'Orcia. All this took place while a few miles away the Romanesque and Gothic styles continued to hold sway at, for example, the minute and wholly delightful village of San Quirico or at Montalcino, the home of the Brunello, the most noble and expensive of Italian wines, a veritable nectar for the disciples of Bacchus. A visit to one of the cellars is a must. The owners are usually only too happy to offer a taste of the fruit of painstakingly tended and precious vineyards. Wine shops abound along the remarkably evocative streets of the town. Each bottle,

130-131 Argentario is an exclusive tourist destination and also a paradise for wildlife. The area is green in spite of the scarcity of fresh water and features sharp cliffs that drop off into a transparent sea.

130 bottom left The fortifications found on Monte Argentario are the work of the Pisans and Sienese, anxious to defend the important promontory against the greed of the Saracen pirates.

130 bottom right Each year, in mid-August, Porto Santo Stefano relives its past gloryes with the Palio Marinaro, preceded by a grand parade in Spanish costumes. Nuño Orejón, the Spanish Govenor who in the mid-sixteenth century transformed the seaside village into a fortified town is honored.

131 The name Porto Ercole derives from the mythological figure of Hercules, a symbol of strength. Today the bay, protected by a breakwater, is one of Argentario's most enchanting spots and is surrounded by coastlines of incomparable beauty.

each vintage, each label is a discovery in its own right. Not far from Montalcini lies another compact surprise, Bagno Vignoni, where the principal piazza is an open-air thermal "piscina." Lorenzo il Magnifico and Pius II came here to treat their rheumatism. The village has been saved from a project which would have transformed it into a form of Tuscan Disneyland, but like many other villages of incomparable beauty in the region it risks being abandoned. This is not the case at Montepulciano, which thanks to its strategic position between the Florentine Republic, the States of the Church, and Siena, succeeded in forging artistic influences fundamental to its economic and urban development and became a splendid Renaissance city. The symbol of the town is its magnificent pilgrimage church of the Madonna di San Biagio by Antonio da Sangallo il Vecchio, situated on a knoll where legend has it that the Virgin Mary appeared before two children and a shepherd in 1518. The name of Montepulciano is also known throughout the world thanks to its Vino Nobile, one of the seven guaranteed quality Italian wines. It is but a short step from the wealth of the Chianti hills to the Maremma, a harsh region, maltreated and often overlooked.

One first has to traverse Monte Amiata, the Mountain of Caves as the Romans called it because of its porous nature and abundant springs. It rises in isolation, an extinct volcano where the Quaternary deposits of the siliceous shells of diatoms are extracted in the form of a fossil flour or "moon milk." Deep in the heart of the mountain mercury can also be found. The springs of Amiata supply Siena, Grosseto, and the whole of southern Tuscany down to Viterbo. The mountain is manna for the grim Maremma and its "capital" Grosseto, something of the Cinderella of Tuscan cities, obscured even by the neighboring Massa Marittima. This is in spite of the presence of massive fortified city walls, a monumental complex which has earned Grosseto a reputation as a minor version of Lucca, an honor for a city which prior to improvements was considered so unattractive that to live there was considered a form of punishment. It is probably not widely known that up to the last century the public offices of the "lower province of Siena" were transferred to Scansano in the summer months.

This was the so-called "estatura," a prudent migration to avoid an epidemic of malaria among the loyal civil servants. In an even earlier age convicts were faced with a choice: imprisonment in the Maschio at Volterra, or forced labor in the Maremma, and the freedom to die of malaria.

There followed bombardments and subsequent reconstruction which, over the course of a few decades, has increased the original dimensions of the city fifteen-fold. It is worth pausing, at least for a while, if only to look at the ruins which bear testimony to the succession of masters and peoples: the Etruscan

132 Giannutri, the southernmost of the islands in the Tuscan archipelago, features the notable remains of a large Roman villa which perhaps belonged to the Domizi Enobarbi family. Roman remains have also been found on the sea bed below the crystal clear water.

132-133 Elba, the largest of the islands in the Tuscan archipelago, was held by the Etruscans, the Greeks, the Romans, and the Lombards before passing to the Republic of Pisa. Its destiny has been determined by its beauty, its strategic position, and also by its considerable natural resources.

133 bottom left Mediterranean maquis thrives on the rocks of the island of Giglio, alternating with minuscule sandy beaches.

133 bottom right Capraia, standing a long way out from the coast (one of the reasons for which it was chosen as a penal colony), attracted arrows of Dante's ire against the Pisan gentlemen.

134-135 The island of Capraia is of extreme geological interest and is generally composed of volcanic rocks with flows of andesite, tufa, breccia, and basaltic rocks. Its name derives from the wild goats found there.

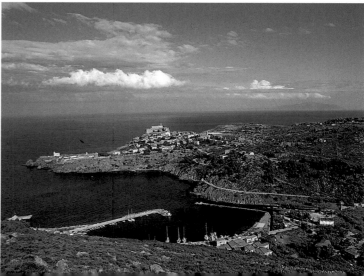

136-137 These are the **butteri**, *the cowboys or gauchos of Italy. Almost inseparable from their horses and the herds they tend, they were once the kings of the Maremma but condemned to labor in a harsh climate, infested with malaria, the curse of the area up until the last century. The* **butteri** *still survive and at the village fairs, or at branding time one can see that they are still as rugged as they were at the beginning of the twentieth century when they successfully met the challenge of the legendary Buffalo Bill, touring Italy at the time.*

137

138 bottom In the maze of vegetation which characterizes the Maremma Natural Park, the wild boar, the King of the Maquis, still reigns. One can also find traces of the last remaining wild cats, as well as porcupines, lynxes, pheasants, foxes, and weasels.

walls, the Roman basilica, and the paleochristian cathedral. One can walk around the ring of green created within the fortified walls in the first half of the nineteenth century, a meeting place but also a dividing line between the humble and generally unloved Grosseto of the "estatura" and the modern city of tower blocks and chaotic planning. The Maremma of bygone days must have been very different, linked to the Amiata by just two roads, and branded by two contrasting curses, drought and stagnant water. Today's Maremma, on the other hand, has been healed and reclaimed and is an upper echelon tourist destination. To tell the truth, the tourists tend to steer clear of the interior, with the exception of Capalbio, a haven for intellectuals and politicians. And yet this is not just a land of "butteri" and parched plains, it is also one of Etruscan remains. Populonia, Rusellae, Vetulonia, and Saturnia are only the most well known centers. And while man's negligence has been responsible for dreadful disasters, the tumulus and aedicule tombs, the interiors, and the environs are infinitely suggestive. The area also boasts its own cities of art such as Pitigliano and Sorano, the cities of tufa, which under the dominion of the Orsini boasted imposing fortifications, and above all Sovana, with its necropolis and the Tomba Ildebranda.

One leaves Tuscany via two protected oases. The Maremma Natural Park, constituted in 1975, extends for around 12 miles along the coast from Tombolo to Talamone, and represents a perfect opportunity to get to know the primitive Maremma. More than simply a green lung, the ancient watchtowers, the remains of the San Rabano monastery, and the estates where the heirs to the "butteri" continue to raise livestock and horses bear witness to a living territory, one in which man exists in contact and in symbiosis with nature. Nature is again the protagonist at the Orbetello Oasis on the salty lagoon with dunes covered with dense Mediterranean maquis, fresh water ponds, and woods. Here the Knight of Italy, egrets, and occasionally flamingos all nest, and you may also spot the nests of the bee-eater. At dusk, the dunes taken on a reddish hue in Argentario in the beautiful village of Porto Ercole. This is a chance for a last salute to art. In the parish church below the Rocca is buried Caravaggio who, following an adventurous life in distant parts, came to end his days in the furthest outpost of Tuscany, the homeland of all artists.

138-139 The Alberese pine forest was at one time a Sienese fief and source of salt. Only following land reclamation were the now flourishing domestic and maritime pines planted. Today there are over 80,000 trees, separated from the sea by just a slim strip of sand.

139 bottom In the Maremma National Park visitors must stay on the paths so as not to invade the realm of the deers and the wild animals.

140-141 The mouth of the Ombrone is the last bastion of the swamps which once guaranteed the Maremma's infamy as an area of mourning and malaria.

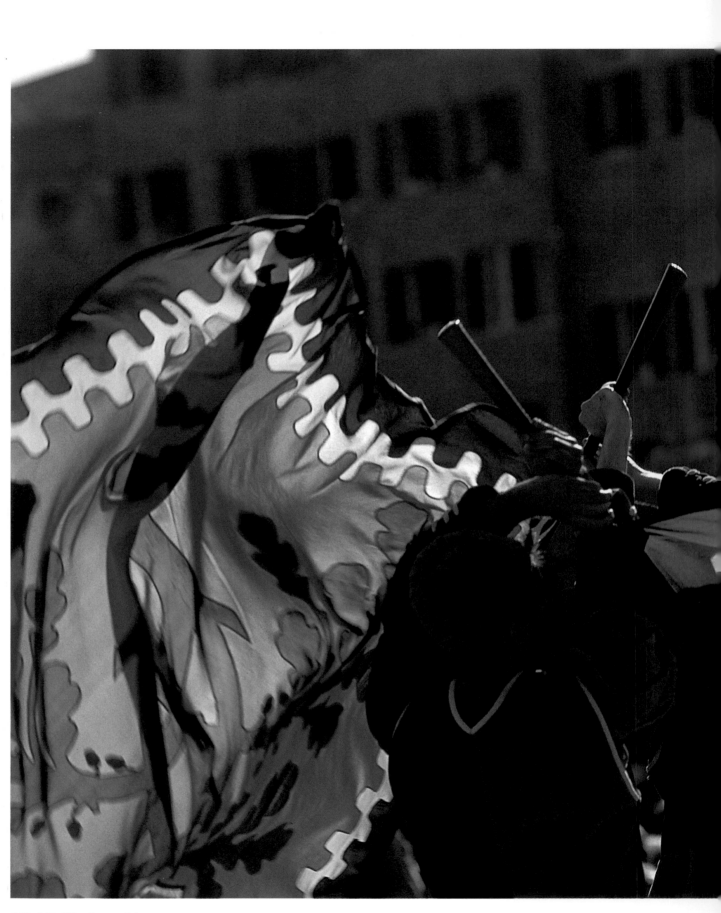

142-143 *The flag-twirlers practice all year round to be ready for their great occasion, the Palio delle Contrade, when they will be called on to demonstrate their skill in front of thousands of spectators.*

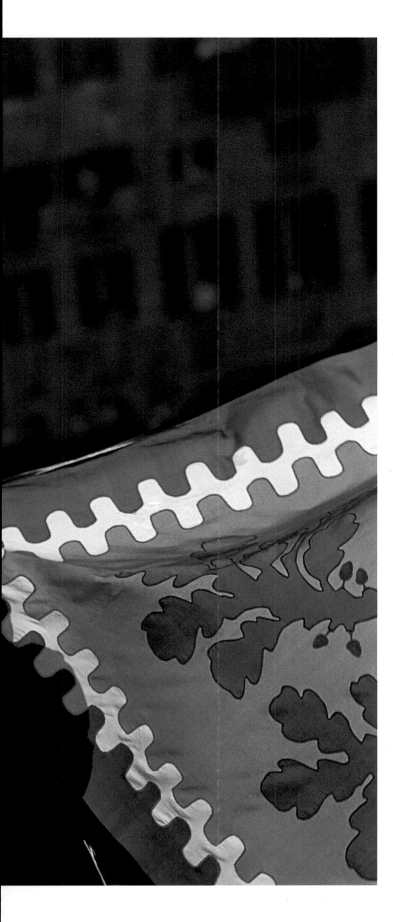

IN THE NAME OF SPORT AND HONOR

How many of the games, and the traditional customs of the Italian people have become part of the patrimony not just of their city of origin, but the whole country, and perhaps even the world? Very few have but of these few, almost all of them originated in Tuscany.

To the prompt of "Siena" a foreigner will probably respond with "Palio," just as "Florence" could be coupled with "Calcio in Costume," and Arezzo with the "Giostra del Saracino." These ancient traditions, to which one could add other events such as Pisa's Gioco del Ponte, or Pistoia's Giostra del'Orso, have often been revived in this century after years of neglect. But the region as a whole is a succession of festivals, often rekindling the competitive spirit of the cities and contrade (neighborhoods) typical of the Middle Ages, and which in the Renaissance was channeled into more relaxed and sporting customs and rituals.

The competitive spirit only rarely spills over into violence, but those watching the "calcio in costume" in Florence are inevitably obliged to support one or the other of the two factions. Neutrality is outlawed, and so are good manners. And to think that this ball game has the noblest of origins: the "sferomachia," as the Crusca dictionary defines the game, descends directly from the Greeks and the Romans (with all due apologies to the British who believe they invented soccer). The game is documented in Florence as far back as the fifteenth century. It was once usually played in the winter and in 1490 even on the frozen Arno, between the Ponte Vecchio and Santa Trinità. The ball weighed ten ounces and the costumes were as comfortable as possible to allow freedom of

movement. But the most unusual aspect of the sport, at least for that era, was that the participants had no need of arms, crossbows, horses, or lances, but just their feet, and on occasion their hands. Nowadays the matches are held in Piazza della Signoria between four teams, each representing one of the city's quarters: San Giovanni in green, Santa Croce in blue, Santa Maria Novella in red, and Santo Spirito in white. The colors are intended to symbolize the four natural elements, the roots and nucleus of everything. Red for fire, green for the land, blue for water and white for air the Calcio in Costume

144-145 There is no holding back for the players in Calcio in Costume in Florence. The match is held in June in Piazza Santa Croce. Four city quarters, San Giovanni, Santa Maria Novella, Santa Croce, and Santo Spirito compete in the games. Although all the participants are called on to swear an oath of fair play, almost anything goes in this intense struggle somewhere between soccer and rugby. And this is despite the fact that the prize is symbolic: a white calf to be eaten all together, as well as the inevitable palio, or banner.

145

is, in reality, a very early form of rugby. The "rules" allow the tackling of one's opponent, with all the ripping of tunics and more or less underhand blows that entails. For the more inexperienced spectators the confusion increases in relation to the number of players involved, twenty-seven per team including "Datori," "Sconciatori," and "Corridori" (Suppliers, Blockers, and Runners) as well as the "Capitano" and the "Alfiere" (standard bearer). The chaos often also involves the Maestro di Campo, who has his work cut out to control all fifty-four of the players. The aim of the game is to score points by throwing the ball into the adversary's end zone, thus effecting a "caccia." A shot at the goal which fails to hit the target results in a half "caccia" for the opposition. And if that seems simple enough, in spite of the "oath of fairness" sworn by the two captains before the start, the matches often deteriorate into saloon-style brawls, with shredded tunics and the dealing of below-the-belt blows accompanied by the roars of the crowd. All that effort is rewarded with a token prize, like all the prizes in these traditional events: a banner and a white calf to be consumed all together at a great banquet.

The origins of Pistoia's Giostra dell'Orso, held in July in honor of San Jacopo, are just as ancient. Originally it was the Palio dei Barberi, a long race through the whole city with a spectacular finish in Piazza del Duomo. It was only following the First World War that the Palio became the Giostra, that is a joust, based above all on skill. The game as it is played today originated in the late 1940's, with considerable historical license being taken. It was even preceded by a rugby match in "primitive" costumes and by a session of mud wrestling. Nowadays the Giostra is held in fifteenth century dress, with much being made of costumed extras, drummers and, flag wavers.

Twelve knights representing the ancient quarters of the city compete on a ring of beaten earth laid down in the piazza as in Siena. The aim is to hit a target in the form of a stylized bear (the same as that which appears in Pistoia's coat of arms) with a lance, trying to get there ahead of one's adversary.

It has to be said that even though it has only recently been revived and had suffered long periods of suspension, the Giostra dell'Orso is getting under the skin of the city. Its inhabitants are rapidly

146 The Scoppio del Carro at Florence is all that remains of the tradition of great allegorical floats that lies somewhere between paganism and Christianity and which enjoyed its greatest period during the Renaissance.

146-147 On the night of June 16th Pisa switches off its street lighting and lights oil lamps to celebrate San Ranieri. The following day the city stages the Gioco del Ponte.

147 bottom The San Ranieri procession at Pisa brings together the faithful from throughout the city in a grandiose illuminated parade rich in emotion, song, and prayer.

turning into convinced "contradists," perhaps harboring a dream of future glory to match that of Siena with live TV broadcasts and competition among the various networks to secure exclusive rights.

Summer is city festival season and Pisa is no exception to the rule. The most passionate and best loved event is that dedicated to the city's patron saint San Ranieri. On the 16th and 17th of August the "Luminaria" lights up the city. On the evening of the 16th the electric street lighting is switched off, and while darkness falls over the city, the banks of the Arno begin to sparkle in the light of thousands of torches. The torches are suspended on the "biancheria," white-painted wooden supports fixed to the facades of the houses and palazzi. At the same time, thousands of minute boats are loaded with candles and launched on the river to float slowly down towards the sea. The following day the festival explodes when the Santa Maria, Sant'Antonio, San Francesco, and San Martino quarters take their places for a regatta culminating in the oarsmen climbing a long pole on the end of which an embroidered banner is fixed.

The Giostra del Saracino at Arezzo, on the other hand, was not held in honor of a saint. In fact, it was once held to suitably celebrate an important event or to honor an illustrious guest. The revived festival held today differs from the traditional event in that originally any knight could compete, while now the protagonists are the jousters representing the various city quarters. The rituals preceding the event are typical of the various Tuscan palio. In the morning a herald announces the program, followed by a parade of squires and drummers. In the afternoon the arms and the contestants receive the blessing of the parish churches in the various quarters, while the flag wavers perform in Piazza Grande. The actual Giostra is fought by two contestants jousting against an effigy of a Saracen king.

When struck, the effigy swings its lead-weighted whip and the knight has to be ready to dodge its blows. Apart from a few bruises he can also acquire penalty points. The list could go on and on as a giostra, a festival, or a tournament, with more or less reliably documented origins, is held in virtually all Tuscan towns and villages.

However, none of these events could ever hope to exceed the Palio of Siena in terms of fame or excitement.

In recent years animal rights activists have railed against the race, fearing maltreatment of the horses, their improper use, and the cruel destiny which, occasionally, leads to them becoming sacrificial victims of the collective passion. The Sienese argue that their foremost interest is the well-being of the steed on which the fate of the contrada rests. After the assignment by ballot, the horses cannot be replaced, and they are treated, spoiled, and watched over like the heir to a throne. One of the contrada's trusted men will sleep in the stall together with the horse. In the three days preceding the race veterinary surgeons are the most sought-after men in the city. Finally, at the end of their career the ageing or injured animals are pensioned off in the beautiful Sienese hills. Arguments apart, everything imaginable has been said and written about the Palio delle Contrade. The rules which govern it, which in their present form date back to the seventeenth century, are severe and it is doubtful whether there is a single Sienese who would want to change the slightest thing. An important role is played by chance which decides which ten of the city's seventeen contrade will participate in the event. And, as we have already seen, it is chance which assigns the horses. The jockey, on the other hand, is chosen, paid and controled by the contrada. Certain names have become part of Palio legend, such as those of Aceto or Andrea Meloni, winner of the record number of races this century. In the past money was a significant factor as the jockeys were in a position to corrupt their adversaries, but nowadays it appears that the thirst for victory is the ruling passion. The contrada knows how to reward the man responsible for its success. Nevertheless, the role of the jockey is of secondary importance. It is the horse who wins. Its rider may well finish on the floor, thrown against the mattresses padding the fearful San Martino corner. He will receive the necessary treatment, but with no undue sympathy.

This is all part of the intimate internal life of the contrade. The spectators at the Palio see nothing but a riot of colors, sounds, and merrymaking. The festival begins in the morning with a mass celebrated by the archbishop on the Piazza, followed by a rather unenthusiastic trial race. No one wants to risk laming their horse, and rather than gallop,

149 The Regata delle
Repubbliche Marinare:
a celebration of the glorious
era in which Pisa contended
for domination of the seas
against Venice, Genoa, and
Amalfi. Only the rivalry
remains from the struggles
of the past, but it is enough
to arouse the crowd and
encourage the participants.

they trot. *Another blessing is given in the*
afternoon, in the local church of the contrada.
The inhabitants all gather round the horse and
rider to hear the words of the priest: "Go and
return victorious!"

In the meantime the tourists gather in Piazza del
Campo. The rich and fortunate sit in the stands or
on the balconies while the others squeeze into the
arena, trying to cope with the heat, the pushing, and
the tension. As the sun slowly begins to set,
tingeing the palazzi *a deep red, the bells of the*
Torre del Mangia ring out and the parade begins
to move. It is then the turn of the starter who tries
to bring the bareback-ridden horses into line
between two ropes before starting the race.
It lasts just a few minutes, but those who have seen
it even just once remember it as a moment frozen
in time in which one struggles even to breathe.
The whole of Siena holds its breath before
exploding in a scream of joy or desperation.
Sportsmanship has no place here: winning is what
counts. Rival contrade *do not shake and forget and*
there are no consoling pats on the back. They meet up
in the evening, however, at great tables to discuss,
laugh, and argue.

The winning contrada *saves a place for the horse*
too. The other place of honor goes to the palio,
the banner painted each year by a different artist,
preferably Sienese.

150-151 The Maestro di
Campo directs the Giostra
del Saracino at Arezzo.
Once the event was organized
to honor illustrious visitors,
princes, and sovereigns.
Today the contest is between
the historic city quarters,
Porta Sant'Andrea, Porta
Crucifera, Porta del Foro,
and Porta Santo Spirito, and
is held in Piazza Grande.

SIENA'S SPORTING SOUL

152-153 The flag twirlers, together with the squires, crossbowmen, and pages, participate in the costumed parade preceding the Palio at Siena. It is a great honor for these boys to hurl their contrada's colors into the air. Each contrada has its own colors, traditions, and even museums dedicated to past editions of the Palio in which you can admire precious flags and banners. The illustrations show the emblems of some of the seventeen contrade: Dragon, Giraffe, Hedgehog, Tower, Tortoise, Panther, Wave, Wolf, and Snail.

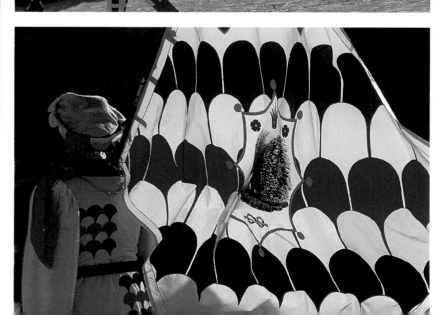

154-155 The Palio at Siena does not last just a few minutes, but a whole year. On the morning of the great day each contrada *accompanies the horse which it has been assigned* to the parish blessing, before the historical parade in Piazza del Campo. The costumes, the arms, and the decorations are perfect replicas of the medieval items.

156-157 The San Martino corner is the most dangerous. Horses and jockeys often see their races end here to the anguish of their supporters. The mattresses do little to attenuate the pain of defeat.

158 Three nail-biting minutes and then one section of the city explodes with joy, while the others despair. The **palio**, painted each year by a different artist, almost always Sienese, is taken up by the contradists and kissed, touched, and praised.

159 After all the trepidation, the winners celebrate with a great banquet. The guest of honor is the horse, the day's real hero.

160 The title of the fountain by Bartolomeo Ammannati in Piazza della Signoria in Florence is Neptune's Chariot. *But the Florentines all know it as* il Biancone.

PHOTO CREDITS